Everyone bringing a healthcare innovation to market needs an early adoption commercialization strategy. Contact Dr. Roxie Mooney via email at roxie@legacy-dna.com. Mention "CoIQ20" in the email subject line to receive a free 20-minute strategy session.

How Health Innovators Maximize Market Success

Strategies to Launch and Commercialize Healthcare Innovations

Dr. Roxie Mooney

**Foreword by
Dr. Joseph C. Kvedar**

THiNKaha®

An Actionable Business Journal

E-mail: info@thinkaha.com
20660 Stevens Creek Blvd., Suite 210
Cupertino, CA 95014

Please go to
http://aha.pub/HealthcareInnovations
to read this AHAbook and to share the
individual AHAmessages that resonate with you.

Published by THiNKaha®
20660 Stevens Creek Blvd., Suite 210,
Cupertino, CA 95014
https://thinkaha.com
E-mail: **info@thinkaha.com**

First Printing: October 2019
Hardcover ISBN: 978-1-61699-337-5   1-61699-337-5
Paperback ISBN: 978-1-61699-336-8   1-61699-336-7
eBook ISBN: 978-1-61699-338-2   1-61699-338-3
Place of Publication: Silicon Valley, California, USA
Paperback Library of Congress Number: 2019911619

Trademarks

Warning and Disclaimer

Acknowledgements

Dr. Rocky Dwyer and Dr. Melvia Scott: The research that grounds this book would not have been possible without your support in my doctoral journey at Walden University. You encouraged me to finish strong when I wanted to give up. I might be in ABD status if it wasn't for you.

Leo Mooney: Just when you think I've accomplished all my dreams, there I go with another one. You have always been super supportive of my educational and career aspirations. I am grateful for your understanding, encouragement, and unceasing prayers. Thanks for being my biggest fan.

Granny: I appreciate the impact you've had on my life. You taught me generosity, perseverance, and instilled in me a strong sense of confidence. Those early days of me selling Avon with you at two years old paid off. Because of you, I believed I could and that I would. I am more grateful for you than I could ever express.

Aunt Lynne: You taught me what it means to be a woman. Fearless. Independent. Comfortable being me. I miss you every day.

Amanda Gaid, Brenda Barham, and Wendy Bacigalupi: To the writers at Legacy DNA, thank you for being a part of the living laboratory of all things CoIQ—from the early stages of my doctoral journey where these ideas were just seedlings to the full bloom of the CoIQ early adoption commercialization strategy blueprint, the CoIQ with Dr. Roxie video and podcast show, and the publication of this book. The truth is that I am not exactly sure where my thinking ends and yours begins. We have spent so much time scrutinizing these concepts together. Thank you, friends.

Amy McIntyre: You make everything beautiful. Your illustrations bring my thoughts to life and help our audiences better understand the world of commercialization of innovation (CoI).

Clients: Each of you has taught me so much about what it takes to transform an idea into a viable business. I am deeply honored and humbled to share the journey of building and growing your business with you.

Max Traylor and Katrina Busselle: Three simple yet life-changing words come to mind: digital, scalable, and residual. You are responsible for helping me scale our business and productize my expertise. I can never thank you enough for the push to do more with less.

Stacie Ruth: What a wild ride—being the first client to experience our CoIQ Early Adoption Commercialization Strategy blueprint. You challenged me, validated product-market fit, and inspired new ideas to make me and the process better. Looking back, I couldn't have had a better pilot partner.

Arete Sisters: Oh to be truly known, accepted, and valued. The space we've shared over the years has shaped my heart and mind in more ways than you can imagine. So many conversations about learning and growing together as business women. I am inspired by your commitment to use your influence for the greater good, and I'm grateful to be in your company.

Dedication

For every health innovator who wants to increase their chances of market success.

How to Read a THiNKaha® Book
A Note from the Publisher

The AHAthat/THiNKaha series is the CliffsNotes of the 21st century. These books are contextual in nature. Although the actual words won't change, their meaning will every time you read one as your context will change. Be ready, you will experience your own AHA moments as you read the AHA messages™ in this book. They are designed to be stand-alone actionable messages that will help you think about a project you're working on, an event, a sales deal, a personal issue, etc., differently. As you read this book, please think about the following:

1. It should only take 15–20 minutes to read this book the first time out. When you're reading, write in the underlined area one to three action items that resonate with you.
2. Mark your calendar to re-read this book again in 30 days.
3. Repeat step #1 and mark one to three more AHA messages that resonate. They will most likely be different than the first time. BTW: this is also a great time to reflect on the AHA messages that resonated with you during your last reading.

After reading a THiNKaha book, marking your AHA messages, re-reading it, and marking more AHA messages, you'll begin to see how these books contextually apply to you. AHAthat/THiNKaha books advocate for continuous, lifelong learning. They will help you transform your AHAs into actionable items with tangible results until you no longer have to say AHA to these moments—they'll become part of your daily practice as you continue to grow and learn.

Mitchell Levy, The AHA Guy at AHAthat
publisher@thinkaha.com

THiNKaha®

Contents

Foreword

How many times have you heard a story about a great idea, exciting product, or a disruptive business that never got off the ground? Sadly, we're hearing about these market failures more and more. According to various estimates, 70 percent to 90 percent of startups fail, and that is already a selected set, because they have crossed the threshold of incorporation. Think of all the ideas that never even make it that far! How can you avoid that pitfall? Certainly, experience is the best teacher, but I am also a fan of Santayana's famous quote: "Those who fail to study history are doomed to repeat it." In other words, there are ways to be thoughtful and strategic as you undertake efforts to commercialize any innovation.

For those who find themselves in the critical phase of launching a business or new product, Dr. Roxie Mooney's book, *How Health Innovators Maximize Market Success*, is a must-read. Roxie has years of experience advising companies on the fundamentals of launching a company, product-market fit, successful pilots, and of course, strategy development. The intertwined relationship between marketing and strategy is a pervasive theme in this book — and in Roxie's work. So, as you might expect, her book is chock-full of lessons learned, to guide an entrepreneur though the gauntlet of commercialization of a healthcare business.

Most of the entrepreneurs who come to me for advice are building businesses at the intersection of health and technology. This is a particularly delicate dance. Technologists are used to quick product cycles and iterative development with lots of audience interaction. Healthcare practitioners are much more reserved and careful, as we take an oath to "do no harm." These two cultures can clash, and when they do, the result is often failure. Guiding entrepreneurs through these early stages takes experience and instinct, and Roxie has both, as evidenced by the wisdom shared in this book. If I'd had this book to read, I would have avoided a number of missteps.

An example that comes to mind involves our evolving understanding of the use of wearables and tracking data in the management of chronic illness. I am a quantitative person and enjoy setting measurable goals and tracking progress. You can imagine how excited I was when the first wave of connected health sensors hit the market (e.g., Fitbit and Withings, to name a few). Because I was so attracted to this new way of managing health, I assumed our patients would be and that the ages-long challenge of health behavior change would be easily won. With no market research and this core belief, I launched a company that never gained traction. We not only learned how difficult it is, in this era, to get consumers' attention but also how weak of a motivator tracking data is. I'm sure we could have short cut all of that by doing some thoughtful market research ahead of time. These lessons learned are covered in multiple places in Roxie's book.

She starts right out with a deep dive into the difference between commercialization and launch. This is an important insight for anyone starting a business, particularly so in healthcare. The next section covers the notion of developing and constantly re-evaluating strategy. Here, she urges entrepreneurs to create a flexible, iterative, and data-centric commercialization framework. This is wonderful advice for the rapid pace of movement and change that startups face today.

Another important and oft-overlooked consideration is timing: should one be first to market, a fast follower, or late entrant? Frequently, individuals choose to launch when the product is ready, not thinking through the implications of when to launch a product. Roxie covers this dilemma nicely in Section IV.

A related personal anecdote involves the launch of our online second opinion program at Partners HealthCare in 2001. At that time, most people viewed the internet as a place to post your brochure. The idea of doing substantive work online was just beginning to be contemplated. We hired one of the big consulting firms to develop the business plan for us, so we thought we were on solid footing when we launched. We missed in two major ways, however. One was the marketing requirements, or what Roxie calls, "rising above the noise" (Section VII). We learned that launching a website is like printing your name in the phone book. Unless someone wants to find it, it will not be found. Second, to the point of leader versus fast follower, etc., our vantage point in academia is to always be first. The currency of academic advancement is being the first to make a discovery. As a large organization, we had the luxury of funding the online second opinion program internally for many years before it was financially sustainable, so being first did not hurt us. If we were investor-funded, we would have gone out of business, as the market was just not ready for online second opinions in 2001. Fast forward to the middle of this decade, when companies like Grand Rounds and Best Doctors began to flourish. Market timing is critical.

Healthcare markets are often complex. Many times, the person paying the bill is different from the individual receiving the service. This creates complexities in terms of building a market and having multiple stakeholders to please. Roxie's book targets this issue exceptionally well in Sections V and VI. Section VI goes further into the challenges with piloting an intervention. The balance that one has to strike is to get enough piloting done to establish proof-of-concept, but not so many that resources are diluted and no one signs up to be a scaling customer.

It is so important in our information-overload age to get noticed or to rise above the noise. Section VII is devoted exclusively to this challenge and the nuances of building a winning communications strategy. The final sections cover branding and co-creation, and the book wraps up with a useful list of survival tips every startup should review.

I am privileged to meet lots of entrepreneurs and to have the opportunity to advise a number of them. While my advice mostly comes from experience, with the publication of this book, I have a new tool to offer my advisees. Roxie Mooney's book will walk them through the jungle of healthcare startups and commercialization in a sane, readable, and easy-to-understand format.

I've learned from Roxie over the years and with this book, you can too. I am excited to see this work influence the success of a generation of entrepreneurs in healthcare. The industry is in trouble and needs successful innovations. Roxie's book represents an important ingredient in that success. I wish I had this book 15 to 20 years ago to guide me in my entrepreneurial pursuits!

Dr. Joseph C. Kvedar, MD
Vice President, Partners Healthcare

Introduction

One of the very first questions I had to answer in my doctoral journey was, "What business problem did I want to spend the next five to six years on?" As I thought about it, there were two contradicting phenomena that piqued my interest. On one hand, there was an explosion of innovation happening in healthcare. On the other hand, I came across this alarming statistic: 95 percent of innovations brought to market fail to reach any adequate level of customer acceptance or financial performance. How were we going to reconcile this gap? It was at that moment I decided to invest my time and money in learning what strategies health innovators needed to adopt to successfully commercialize their innovations.

Unlike other industries, our quality of life—and our very lives—depend on getting these innovations through the complexities of the commercialization process and the healthcare ecosystem and into the hands of the people who need them most. In many cases, it could be our loved ones' health or even our own at stake.

I wake up each morning thinking about how many technologies and advancements health innovators dream up that end up in a zombie graveyard. It's not that their products don't solve a real problem or aren't superior to competing solutions. It's because commercializing an innovation is hard, especially in healthcare.

If there's a new product idea that could mitigate the healthcare crisis and make our lives better, I'd like to help move these innovations from the zombie realm to the land of the living.

There are nearly 75,000 healthcare innovations in the process of being brought to market. They range from telehealth to connected medical devices, digital therapeutics, remote monitoring tools, on-demand primary care, and many other exciting technology advancements. There are many things that must go right to transform these innovations into profitable businesses.

As health innovators, you have three options. Option 1: Avoid failure. Option 2: Increase your chances of success. Option 3: Maximize market success. Many health innovators are happy if they avoid failure. The ones who truly make a difference in the market are those who have figured out how to maximize their success.

Pyramid of Healthcare Innovation Success

I think of the three aforementioned options much like a pyramid with the most desirable scenario at the top. This helps clarify the meaning of success and its variables.

- **Maximizing Market Success**—Thriving. High amounts of short-term satisfaction and a high number of long-term benefits.

- **Increasing Your Chances of Success**—Sustaining. Possibly interesting in the short term, but not particularly rewarding in the long run.

- **Avoiding Failure**—Surviving. Low amounts of short-term satisfaction and a limited number of long-term benefits.

While there are multiple pitfalls to jump over or maneuver through, my research indicates that health innovators can increase their chances of success by developing an early adoption commercialization strategy—a comprehensive business strategy for how the organization will create, deliver, and capture value, focused specifically on satisfying early adopters. There are five components required for penetrating the early market: timing, targeting, communication, product, and pilot strategies.

This book is written for health innovators who want to discover not only how to avoid failure but also how to implement these key components of an early adoption commercialization strategy. By applying these insights, health innovators will increase their chances of success and ensure that they are making the most of their healthcare innovations.

The following pages are packed with quick and easy-to-read strategic insights to inspire and motivate health innovators toward maximum market success.

Commercial SUCCE$$

Just because your #HealthcareInnovation solves a real problem or is superior to competing solutions doesn't automatically mean you will successfully #**Commercialize** it.

DR. ROXIE MOONEY
http://aha.pub/DrRoxieMooney

Share the AHA messages from this book socially by going to
http://aha.pub/HealthcareInnovations.

Section I

Setting Yourself Up for Commercial Success

Commercializing an innovation in any industry is hard, but it's especially complex in healthcare. Research and experience indicate that even the most promising ideas face an onslaught of commercialization challenges.

There are many forces that can kill an innovation. Confusing the processes of launch and commercialization. Overlooking the early adoption lens. Leading with a technology solution and looking for a problem later. Not figuring out who will pay for the innovation up front. Being in a multi-sided market and confusing who is the user, the buyer, the prescriber, and the influencer, etc. Not seeing the patient as a consumer or viewing them only as a consumer. Not preparing for the long sales cycles inherent to healthcare. Leapfrogging right over strategy and diving right into tactical execution. These are just to name a few. But health innovators are far from hapless and are certainly not helpless. They can indeed control many of these commercialization decisions.

There are also many forces that can drive an innovation. Understanding the difference between launch and commercialization. Developing an early adoption commercialization strategy that includes the five key components required for penetrating the early market: timing, targeting, communications, product, and pilot strategies. Using an evidence-based methodology for making commercialization decisions. Getting expert guidance from a healthcare commercialization strategist. Focusing on early market first. Plus many more that you'll find in this book.

"The team and the process that the team uses to commercialize an innovation is as important as what you're commercializing."—Stacie Ruth, AireHealth
www.drroxie.com/stacie

Watch this video:
http://aha.pub/HealthcareInnovationsS1

1

Just because your #HealthcareInnovation solves a real problem or is superior to competing solutions doesn't automatically mean you will successfully #Commercialize it.

_____

_____

_____

2

Test your #HealthcareInnovation on a bigger scale to understand if it's only you, your neighbor, and your mother who think it's a good idea.

_____

_____

_____

3

Leapfrog over strategy to focus on tactics, and you're doomed. If you want to successfully #Commercialize your #HealthcareInnovation, developing a #Commercialization strategy is essential.

_____

_____

_____

4

#HealthInnovators have three options. Option 1: Avoid failure. Option 2: Increase their chances of success. Option 3: Maximize market success. What is your goal? #Commercialization

_____

_____

_____

5

#Commercialization is the most critical stage of the #HealthcareInnovation process, but it is often the least well-managed stage.

_____

_____

_____

6

An early adoption #Commercialization strategy is a comprehensive business strategy for how an organization will create, deliver, and capture value, focused specifically on satisfying #EarlyAdopters.

_____

_____

_____

7

If you want to successfully #Commercialize your #HealthcareInnovation, start with the problem, not the technology.

_____

_____

_____

8

The target market is not a homogenous group of buyers. Start with an early adoption #Commercialization strategy if you want to successfully #Commercialize your #HealthcareInnovation.

_____

_____

_____

9

95% of innovations brought to market fail to reach an adequate level of customer acceptance and profitability. How will you beat the odds with your #HealthcareInnovation?

_____

_____

_____

10

There are 3 lenses of innovation: 1) desirability (people want it), 2) feasibility (we can actually do it), and 3) viability (we won't go broke). If you can't validate these 3, you need to rethink your #Commercialization strategy.

_____

_____

11

Success in the mainstream market depends on success with #EarlyAdopters. If you are not successful with them, you will not be successful over the long term. #Commercialization

_____

_____

_____

12

Successful #HealthInnovators have strategies for all 5 components of their early adoption #Commercialization strategy: timing, targeting, communication, product, and pilot strategies.

_____

_____

_____

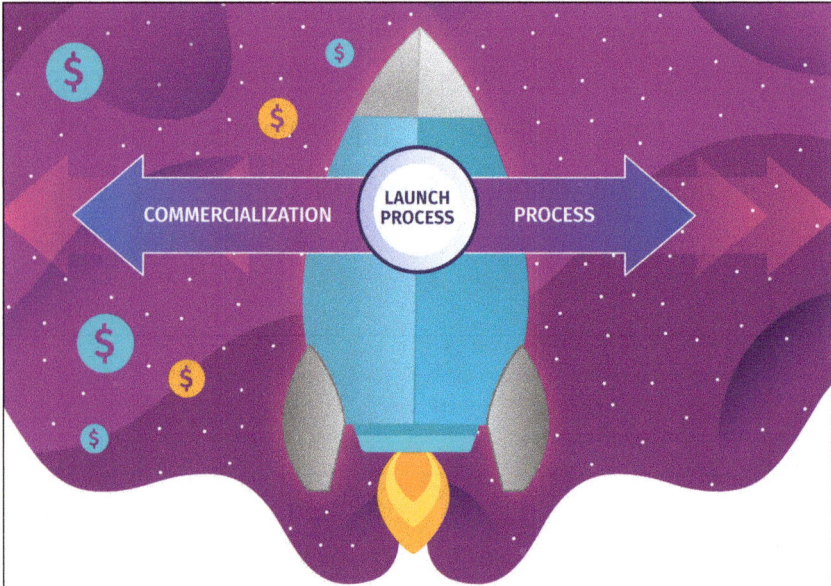

Many #HealthInnovators will launch an #Innovation; **few will #Commercialize it.**

DR. ROXIE MOONEY
http://aha.pub/DrRoxieMooney

Share the AHA messages from this book socially by going to
http://aha.pub/HealthcareInnovations.

Section II

The Difference Between Launching and Commercializing a Healthcare Innovation

Many people use the terms "launch" and "commercialize" interchangeably, but they're different functions of the innovation process. Many new healthcare innovations are launched into the market, but few reach commercial success and generate a profit.

There are two distinguishing factors between launching and commercializing an innovation: the timing and the goal of the initiative. Launching is a much smaller-scale process: it occurs when the innovation is developed and ready for its first release into the market. Commercialization is the holistic process of converting ideas, research, and concepts into viable products that obtain customer acceptance, cross into mainstream adoption, and ultimately generate a financial return on the innovation.

Launching is critical, of course, but it's actually a subset of commercialization. Once you know the difference between launching and commercialization, it will be easier to effectively plan and strategize your healthcare innovation's launch and commercialization.

Watch this video:
http://aha.pub/HealthcareInnovationsS2

13

Successful #HealthInnovators know the difference between #Launching and #Commercializing a #HealthcareInnovation. They have strategies for both.

_____

_____

_____

14

Developing the #Commercialization strategy takes place long before the #HealthcareInnovation is ready for #Launch and continues long after its initial release.

_____

_____

_____

15

Many #HealthInnovators will launch an #Innovation; few will #Commercialize it.

_____

_____

_____

16

Successful #HealthInnovators need to develop their #Commercialization strategy much earlier than the #Launch and product development phases.

_____

_____

_____

17

The goal of #Launching a #HealthcareInnovation is to build awareness and create demand vs. the goal of #Commercialization being to increase customer adoption and profitability from the innovation.

_____

_____

_____

18

#Launching is critical, but it is a subset of #Commercialization. It occurs when the #HealthcareInnovation is developed and ready for its first release into the market.

_____

_____

_____

19

#Commercialization decisions need to be made before your #HealthcareInnovation is ready to launch.

_____

_____

_____

20

#Commercialization is the process of converting ideas, research, and concepts into viable #HealthcareInnovations that obtain customer acceptance, cross into mainstream adoption, and generate financial return.

_____

_____

21

#Commercializing a #HealthcareInnovation doesn't start with creating a logo and a website.

_____

_____

_____

22

There are 2 ways to measure #Commercial success:
1) the degree of customer acceptance and
2) the financial performance achieved by the #HealthcareInnovation.

_____

_____

_____

23

Remember, no matter how much money you invest in developing your #HealthcareInnovation, you must allocate resources for #Launching the product and building awareness.

_____

_____

_____

24

How a #HealthInnovator understands and leverages the #Launch and #Commercialization processes can either set them on a course to failure or a path for success.

_____

_____

_____

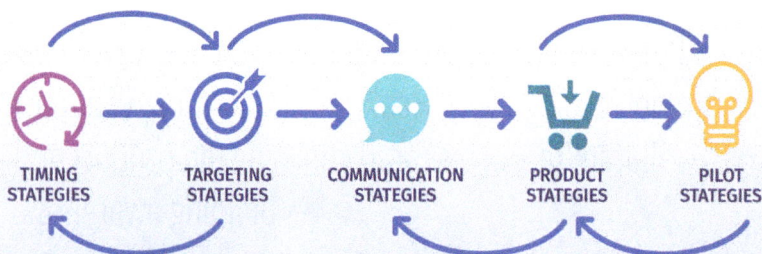

TIMING STATEGIES → TARGETING STATEGIES → COMMUNICATION STRATEGIES → PRODUCT STATEGIES → PILOT STATEGIES

There are no shortcuts to a winning strategy.
Be prepared to change your
#Commercialization decisions until you
identify product market fit and your most
profitable #Commercialization strategy.
#StrategyDevelopment

DR. ROXIE MOONEY
http://aha.pub/DrRoxieMooney

Share the AHA messages from this book socially by going to
http://aha.pub/HealthcareInnovations.

Section III

Managing the Strategy Development Process Is Essential for Commercial Success

The days of developing robust, static strategic plans are gone. It's just not effective anymore. Elements like customer needs and wants, technology, market trends, the competitive landscape, and the way customers connect and interact with brands change way too fast.

This is especially true for startups, when the future is hard to read and the most profitable strategy is not yet known. An emergent strategy needs to be developed as the right ideas surface. A goal of the commercialization strategy development process is to get innovators to think differently and deeper about their assumptions and connect insights between disparate parts of the commercialization process to make sure the most effective early adoption strategy is developed.

That's why it's important for health innovators to have a flexible, iterative, and data-centric commercialization framework—to continuously identify the most impactful strategies, implement them incrementally, evaluate how they perform and optimize based on performance data. Then, do it all over again.

"You've got to fail, you've got to learn, you've got to change, and you've got to grow."
—Robbie Cape, 98point6
www.drroxie.com/robbie

Watch this video:
http://aha.pub/HealthcareInnovationsS3

25

Expect the development of your early adoption #Commercialization strategy to be an iterative process; it's not static or fixed.

_____

_____

_____

26

Successful #HealthInnovators have a thinking partner to help them think differently and deeper about assumptions and bring them back to reality. #StrategyDevelopment

_____

_____

_____

27

#HealthInnovators reduce their chances of market failure when they have an evidence-based blueprint for making #Commercialization decisions.

_____

_____

_____

28

Successful #HealthInnovators don't overinvest in the #HealthcareInnovation and leave limited resources for bringing the innovation to market. #StrategyDevelopment

_____

_____

_____

29

A solid #StrategyDevelopment process for #Commercializing a #HealthcareInnovation is agile and flexible. #HealthInnovators need to continuously build, test, and iterate #Commercialization decisions based on data and analysis.

_____

_____

_____

30

As you go to market, look for new useful insights to optimize your #Commercialization strategy. #StrategyDevelopment

_____

_____

_____

31

Managing an emergent #StrategyDevelopment process requires focus. #HealthInnovators need to prioritize the things that matter.

_____

_____

_____

32

There are no shortcuts to a winning strategy. Be prepared to change your #Commercialization decisions until you identify product-market fit and your most profitable #Commercialization strategy. #StrategyDevelopment

_____

_____

33

In the beginning, the future is hard to read, and the most profitable #Commercialization strategy is not yet known. #HealthInnovators need to craft an emergent strategy as the right ideas surface. #StrategyDevelopment

_____

_____

_____

34

Having a blueprint that shows how all your decisions influence the #Commercialization process helps you better manage the #StrategyDevelopment of your #HealthcareInnovation.

_____

_____

_____

35

Successful #HealthInnovators make sure that they are not only planning to launch a product but are also developing an early adoption #Commercialization strategy. #StrategyDevelopment

----

36

Successful #HealthInnovators use agile strategy sprints to determine which questions to answer, which assumptions to validate, and which strategic moves to make. #StrategyDevelopment

----

37

Successful #HealthInnovators make users and buyers a part of their decision making early in the #StrategyDevelopment process, not an afterthought.

_____

_____

_____

38

As a #HealthInnovator, the first goal is to solve problems and satisfy early adopters, not to please everyone in the market. #StrategyDevelopment

_____

_____

_____

Primary Entry Timing Strategies

FIRST MOVER

FAST FOLLOWER

LATE ENTRANT

RISK

Being first-to-market doesn't automatically equal a competitive advantage or ensure profits. Successful #HealthInnovators choose the best **#TimingStrategy** for their specific situation.

DR. ROXIE MOONEY
http://aha.pub/DrRoxieMooney

Share the AHA messages from this book socially by going to
http://aha.pub/HealthcareInnovations.

Section IV

Timing Strategies: Early Mover, Follower, or Late Entrant

When it comes to timing strategies, many health innovators default to, "I'm going to market when the new product is ready to launch," without much purpose and intention about their order of entry into a new or existing space. Or, they assume that being first-to-market will automatically equal a competitive advantage and ensured profits.

Understanding key timing concepts, pitfalls to watch out for, and the unique characteristics of the company's strategic intent, risk exposure, resource capabilities, partner relationships, market conditions, and industry evolution increases an innovator's potential for market success.

There are advantages and disadvantages to the three primary market entry timing strategies of early mover, follower, and late entrant. Knowing these insights and understanding how these factors influence an innovator's competitive advantage affects market success and drives the timing decisions made by innovators.

Watch this video:
http://aha.pub/HealthcareInnovationsS4

39

The #TimingStrategy is a fundamental decision for when a #HealthInnovator launches a new innovation into the market. Choosing the best time to #Commercialize is a key success factor.

_____

_____

_____

40

Carefully planning your #TimingStrategy can help you successfully #Commercialize your #HealthcareInnovation.

_____

_____

_____

41

There are 4 factors to consider when choosing your #TimingStrategy: 1) industry and product trends, 2) the nature of the #HealthcareInnovation, 3) the intensity of the competition, and 4) resources and capabilities.

_____

_____

_____

42

Just because a #HealthInnovator can be first-to-market doesn't mean they should. What do you think is the best #TimingStrategy for you?

_____

_____

_____

43

Being first-to-market doesn't automatically equal a competitive advantage or ensure profits. Successful #HealthInnovators choose the best #TimingStrategy for their specific situations.

_____

_____

_____

44

Early movers are the first #HealthInnovators to introduce #HealthcareInnovations that create a new market or major subfield within a market. Is being an early mover your #TimingStrategy?

_____

_____

_____

45

Early movers can attain recognition and reputation. Their brand can be synonymous with the category of their #HealthcareInnovation if they #Commercialize it right. #TimingStrategy

---

46

Followers are #HealthInnovators who enter a known #HealthcareInnovation market. Are you an early mover or a follower? There are cases to be made for both. #TimingStrategy

_____

_____

_____

47

Followers have several advantages: coming into an established market category, seeing the mistakes made by the first entrant, and being able to fill the gaps between the current solution and buyer's needs or wants. #TimingStrategy

_____

_____

_____

48

Late entrants are #HealthInnovators who enter a mature market. Is being a late entrant your #TimingStrategy? Being a late entrant doesn't mean you're a loser. Do what's best for your innovation.

_____

_____

_____

49

Late entrants get a "free ride" from early mover investments, often bear lower innovation costs, and have access to more market knowledge. #TimingStrategy #HealthcareInnovation

_____

_____

_____

50

Successful #HealthInnovators understand the importance of knowing when they're going to market and how it will shape their #Commercial success. #TimingStrategies

_____

_____

_____

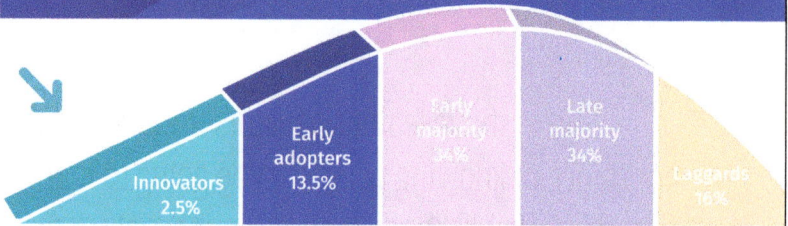

Diffusion of Innovation

Innovators 2.5%

Early adopters 13.5%

Early majority 34%

Late majority 34%

Laggards 16%

A one-size-fits-all targeting strategy is not an effective approach. Successful #HealthInnovators target and cater to a specific audience. Do you? #EarlyAdopters

DR. ROXIE MOONEY

http://aha.pub/DrRoxieMooney

Share the AHA messages from this book socially by going to
http://aha.pub/HealthcareInnovations.

Section V

Targeting Early Adopters for Your Commercialization Strategy

Audience targeting, or market selection, is the foundation of all commercialization decisions. Targeting is important because commercial success strongly depends on the company's knowledge and understanding of the group(s) of customers who share similar needs and buying behaviors and which segments are more likely to adopt the innovation. For example, who has an unmet need or job to be done? The answer can help you hone in on the right markets and segments.

Health innovators who fail to produce a positive post-purchase attitude among early adopters are those who fail to target a specific market segment. Audience segmentation is particularly critical for health innovators where multi-side markets are common, business models are often B2B2C, and buyers are often different from the users with distinct needs to make a purchasing decision. Many innovators wrestle with identifying all the various players and figuring out the right business model.

Watch this video:
http://aha.pub/HealthcareInnovationsS5

51

#HealthInnovators can ensure that their launch becomes successful by targeting #EarlyAdopters.

_____

_____

_____

52

The target market of a #HealthcareInnovation consists of: 1) #EarlyAdopters and 2) the mainstream market. Whom are you targeting for your launch? The answer should be early adopters.

_____

_____

_____

53

#HealthInnovators are more likely to have success in the mainstream market if they: 1) target #EarlyAdopters, 2) influence them to buy, and 3) make sure they are satisfied.

_____

_____

_____

54

The launch success of your #HealthcareInnovation strongly depends on your knowledge and understanding of the characteristics, needs, and buying intentions of #EarlyAdopters.

_____

_____

_____

55

Successful #HealthInnovators target #EarlyAdopters because they drive adoption in the mainstream market.

_____

_____

_____

56

Successful #HealthInnovators target #EarlyAdopters first because they know that this market segment is key to diffusing the #HealthcareInnovation within the mainstream market.

_____

_____

_____

57

The launch strategy process begins with understanding your #EarlyAdopters and how to properly introduce your #HealthcareInnovation to them.

_____

_____

_____

58

Successful #HealthInnovators know that success in the mainstream market depends on success with #EarlyAdopters.

_____

_____

_____

59

Successful #HealthInnovators know that the launch message they use for #EarlyAdopters is different from the mainstream market. Are you getting out the right message?

_____

_____

_____

60

Successful #HealthInnovators ensure that their launch message resonates with #EarlyAdopters because they are the first potential buyers of the #HealthcareInnovation and help stimulate diffusion.

_____

_____

_____

61

Product-market fit means being in a good market with a product that can satisfy that market. — Marc Andreessen #EarlyAdopters #HealthcareInnovation

_____

_____

_____

62

A one-size-fits-all targeting strategy is not an effective approach. Successful #HealthInnovators target and cater to a specific audience. Do you? #EarlyAdopters

_____

_____

_____

Big brands don't always equal #HealthcarePilot success or sales. In fact, sometimes, #HealthInnovators should say "no" to the big players and seek out small-to-medium pilot partners.

DR. ROXIE MOONEY
http://aha.pub/DrRoxieMooney

Share the AHA messages from this book socially by going to
http://aha.pub/HealthcareInnovations.

Section VI

Setting Up Your Pilot for Success as Part of Your Commercialization Strategy

It's a sad story that plays out all too often. A healthcare tech startup is ready to bring an innovation to market. Before the company can earn a reputation of trust and credibility—for commercialization—it needs proof of clinical efficacy and safety and possibly final product enhancements based on its performance in the real world.

Many companies partner with a prospective customer for a pilot to remedy this challenge. Healthcare innovation pilot programs are a common and often effective route for securing early adopters. However, the costly and prolonged nature of a pilot and the innately cautious and risk-averse traits of the healthcare industry can turn them into death traps for innovators, especially for a radical innovation.

"Death by pilot" can be a tragedy for health innovators, as well as patients and the healthcare systems that never get the chance to benefit from the innovation in the first place.

"If someone is using a solution that does not work in place of something that we know does, there's a risk there. Evidence is what helps people de-risk." —Dr. Kate Wolin, Coeus Health
www.drroxie.com/kate

Watch this video:
http://aha.pub/HealthcareInnovationsS6

63

#HealthInnovators can earn trust and credibility through successful #HealthcarePilots. A successful pilot can be a positive move toward #Commercial success.

_____

_____

_____

64

If your #HealthcareInnovation doesn't address a problem that is a priority for the #HealthcarePilot partner, it's time to explore other partners.

_____

_____

_____

65

Plan for #HealthcarePilots and clinical studies. It is difficult to gain customer adoption if you cannot validate the safety and clinical efficacy of your #HealthcareInnovation in the real world.

_____

_____

_____

66

Big brands don't always equal #HealthcarePilot success or sales. In fact, sometimes, #HealthInnovators should say "no" to the big players and seek out small-to-medium-sized pilot partners.

_____

_____

_____

67

#HealthInnovators achieve a successful #HealthcarePilot by identifying the KPIs that validate the safety and efficacy of their #HealthcareInnovation before the pilot is launched.

68

Successful #HealthInnovators partner with the early market in their #HealthcarePilot because they are more likely to buy the #HealthcareInnovation in the long run.

69

Connect with multiple team members at all levels within the #HealthcarePilot organization to convert them into champions and ambassadors.

_____

_____

_____

70

Successful #HealthInnovators know that having real-world feedback is important, yet remain cautious in making changes to their #HealthcareInnovation just because a #HealthcarePilot partner said so.

_____

_____

_____

71

Successful #HealthInnovators don't get so excited when a potential #HealthcarePilot partner is interested in their #HealthcareInnovation that they accept unfavorable terms during the pilot negotiation process.

_____

_____

_____

72

Ask #HealthcarePilot participants to share in the costs to ensure that they have a vested interest in the completion of the #HealthcareInnovation.

_____

_____

_____

73

Create a performance-based agreement with the #HealthcarePilot partner up front. If the pilot is a success and the #HealthcareInnovation proves its worth, the pilot partner should commit to buy in advance.

_____

_____

_____

74

Successful #HealthInnovators negotiate sales terms for the end of the #HealthcarePilot in the pilot agreement. Is this a common practice for you?

_____

_____

_____

75

#HealthcarePilot strategies can make or break the success of a #HealthcareInnovation. Take the time to develop your strategies to maximize your return on each pilot relationship.

_____

_____

_____

RISE ABOVE THE NOISE

Successful #HealthInnovators don't underestimate the value of asking doctors, nurses, and patients how to **#RiseAboveTheNoise.**

DR. ROXIE MOONEY
http://aha.pub/DrRoxieMooney

Share the AHA messages from this book socially by going to
http://aha.pub/HealthcareInnovations.

Section VII

How to Rise Above the Noise as Part of Your Commercialization Strategy

There is a great deal of noise in healthcare. If you're launching an innovation, you're in a fight for the eyes and ears of your target audiences, day in and day out. You can guarantee that many brands are vying for the attention of the audience segments you are pursuing. It's a real battle for their focus and attention.

Rising above the noise starts with a clear, concise, and curiosity-invoking value proposition that differentiates your innovation. Innovators need to convince early adopters that their innovation is more valuable, relevant, and worthwhile than everything else that's competing for their finite attention.

Nailing this sounds simple, but it's something that most innovators struggle with. Then, it's about leveraging the latest technology, tactics, and tools to create "now content" and get into the everyday life of your target audience.

"There is a healthcare equivalent to celebrity endorsements. There is a healthcare equivalent to getting buzz on social media. Do not underestimate the value of spending money on PR and marketing, it's really important."
—*Dr. Joseph Kvedar, Partners Healthcare*
www.drroxie.com/joseph

Watch this video:
http://aha.pub/HealthcareInnovationsS7

76

Whether you're the biggest, fastest, richest, smallest, or slowest #HealthInnovator, you need to #RiseAboveTheNoise to achieve launch success.

_____

_____

_____

77

Successful #HealthInnovators stand out among their competitors. Catch the eye of early adopters and make that key impression fast. #RiseAboveTheNoise

_____

_____

_____

78

Remarkable pertains to something that's so amazing, it's worth making remarks about. Is your #Launch strategy remarkable? Does it #RiseAboveTheNoise?

_____

_____

_____

79

Being remarkable and #RisingAboveTheNoise isn't rocket science; it's so simple that most people skip over it. Don't over-complicate it in your #Commercialization strategy. #HealthcareInnovation

_____

_____

_____

80

Having remarkable messaging makes a world of difference in connecting with your early market audience. #RiseAboveTheNoise #HealthcareInnovation

_____

_____

_____

81

Looking to expand your content marketing team? Try talking with the patients, nurses, and healthcare providers that make up your target market. They are the word-of-mouth marketers of tomorrow. #RiseAboveTheNoise

_____

_____

82

Successful #HealthInnovators don't underestimate the value of asking doctors, nurses, and patients how to #RiseAboveTheNoise.

_____

_____

_____

83

#HealthInnovators can #RiseAboveTheNoise by finding out where their early market audiences hang out, connecting with influencers in these spaces, and utilizing them to stimulate diffusion of your #HealthcareInnovation.

_____

_____

84

The secret to #RiseAboveTheNoise and successfully launch your #HealthcareInnovation is positioning, messaging, and coming up with a central theme to which people can authentically connect.

_____

_____

_____

85

When #HealthInnovators leverage unique tactics from other industries, it can differentiate them in their markets. #RiseAboveTheNoise

_____

_____

_____

86

Social media platforms give #HealthInnovators the opportunity to #RiseAboveTheNoise by publishing content that is timely, fresh, and relevant.

_____

_____

_____

87

When #HealthInnovators create timely and relevant content, they create opportunities to participate in conversations about the everyday lives of their target audiences. #RiseAboveTheNoise

_____

_____

_____

88

#HealthInnovators can #RiseAboveTheNoise by executing creative ideas that light up the brand and generate more qualified leads.

_____

_____

_____

89

Make sure your message resonates with early adopters before scaling your marketing program. Have you run A/B tests to validate the proof of concept in your sales and marketing funnel for your #HealthcareInnovation? #RiseAboveTheNoise

_____

_____

90

When your customers speak—through testimonials,
experiences, feedback, and reviews—your adoption
rate will increase and your revenue will grow.
Are you leveraging the voice of your customers to
#RiseAboveTheNoise? #HealthcareInnovation

_____

_____

_____

91

If you want to #RiseAboveTheNoise, your messaging
must focus on the unique characteristics of
early adopters.

_____

_____

_____

Dare to stand out. I. Dare. You.

#Branding

#HealthcareInnovation

DR. ROXIE MOONEY
http://aha.pub/DrRoxieMooney

Share the AHA messages from this book socially by going to
http://aha.pub/HealthcareInnovations.

Section VIII

How Branding Impacts Diffusion of Your Healthcare Innovation

The word "innovation" gets a great deal of lip service in healthcare and for good reason. Innovation can drive growth, boost profits, and slash the competition, not to mention change the world for the better. But when an innovation is not branded, the impact is usually short-lived, if it occurs at all.

Putting "new" or "improved" on a brochure or website is unlikely to create any lasting sense of differentiation. Similarly, an unbranded claim is likely to be interpreted as another example of puffery: "a better workflow" or "a more reliable nebulizer." It is much easier to remember a brand name versus the details of a new offering. To own, diffuse, and fully benefit from an innovation, *you have to build a brand* (as opposed to just giving it a name and logo).

Watch this video:
http://aha.pub/HealthcareInnovationsS8

92

Successful #HealthInnovators understand the impact that good #Branding can have on the #Commercial success of #HealthcareInnovations.

_____

_____

_____

93

#Branding helps diffuse #HealthcareInnovations throughout the market and increases a #HealthInnovator's potential for success.

_____

_____

_____

94

Free your #HealthcareInnovation from the confines of
me-too #Branding and corporate blandness.

_____

_____

_____

95

Compelling #Branding starts with defining and
communicating the unique personality of the business,
not creating a logo.

_____

_____

_____

96

Following the status quo leads only to more of the same. How will target customers believe that your #HealthcareInnovation is a new or better way to solve their problems if your #Branding looks like your competitors'?

_____

_____

_____

97

#Branding helps #HealthInnovators differentiate their businesses authentically and meaningfully from all others.

_____

_____

_____

98

Boring is invisible. No one ever became world famous by blending in, nor did any business. #Branding

_____

_____

_____

99

Dare to stand out. I. Dare. You. #Branding #HealthcareInnovation

_____

_____

_____

100

Use #Branding to connect with the hearts and minds of your early adopters, and you'll reap big rewards.

_____

_____

_____

101

Building a solid relationship with your early market starts with adding human elements to your brand identity: attitude, personality, and values. #Branding

_____

_____

_____

102

Successful #HealthInnovators clearly convey what their #HealthcareInnovation is designed for, how consumers benefit from the product, and why they should spend money on it. #Branding

_____

_____

_____

103

Differentiation is key if your #HealthcareInnovation is to stand out as the only choice in your marketplace. #Branding

_____

_____

_____

104

Over-branding can be fatal. Under-branding can lead to confusion, lack of differentiation, and an overall flop of the #HealthcareInnovation. Are you making sure that your #Branding is just right?

_____

_____

_____

105

Remember, early adopters buy based on emotion, and the mainstream market justifies their purchase based on logic. The #Branding of your #HealthcareInnovation has to touch your audience's emotional and logical sides.

_____

_____

_____

106

Successful #HealthInnovators inspire raving, loyal fans among early adopters to stimulate the diffusion of their #HealthcareInnovation.

_____

_____

_____

Share the AHA messages from this book socially by going to
http://aha.pub/HealthcareInnovations.

Section IX

The Why, How, and When of Co-creation During Product Development

Developing the right product for the right audience is foundational to healthcare innovation, and tapping into the many voices of buyers and users early in the commercialization process is vital.

Patients, physicians, nurses, administrators, etc. often offer hidden insights, inspire new ideas, bring innovators back to reality, and help position innovations for commercial success. They are the product developers, designers, and marketers of tomorrow. Health innovators who want to win must invite them to be active participants in the product innovation process.

Health innovators who develop products with all stakeholders' insights, expectations, and perceived value in mind can make more informed commercialization decisions, better use organizational resources, significantly lower their risk of failure, and boost their chances for success.

"Consider starting with a patient advisory board to involve patients earlier in the product co-creation process." —David Goldsmith, WEGO Health www.drroxie.com/david

"Involve nurses up front in the design and development process to help speed up R&D time and eliminate ideas that won't work." —Dr. Bonnie Clipper, Wambi www.drroxie.com/bonnie

Watch this video:
http://aha.pub/HealthcareInnovationsS9

107

#HealthcareInnovation should not be done in a vacuum. There's incredible value in bringing other people along in the #ProductDevelopment process.

_____

_____

_____

108

Successful #HealthInnovators involve relevant stakeholders in all 5 "Co-s" of the #ProductDevelopment process: co-ideation, co-valuation, co-design, co-test, and co-launch.

_____

_____

_____

109

Product co-creation is not a single event. It's a recurring process throughout the entire company life cycle. #ProductDevelopment

_____

_____

_____

110

Successful #HealthInnovators look at their customers as part of their #ProductDevelopment team throughout the entire commercialization process and product life cycle. Do you?

_____

_____

_____

111

Successful #HealthInnovators don't have a "know-it-all" attitude. Listen and be open to user input to ensure that your #HealthcareInnovation meets the requirements of patients and healthcare professionals.

_____

_____

_____

112

By choosing to co-create with the people whom your #HealthcareInnovation is going to serve, you significantly increase your chances of #Commercial success.

_____

_____

_____

113

Successful #HealthInnovators build co-creation into their #Commercialization strategy.

_____

_____

_____

114

Creating a #ProductDevelopment board that includes the same people who want to use and buy your #HealthcareInnovation boosts the potential for #Commercial success.

_____

_____

_____

115

Involving patients, providers, and other early market customers in the co-creation process can provide #ProductDevelopment insights that #HealthInnovators often miss on their own.

_____

_____

_____

116

Patients, nurses, providers, administrators, and stakeholders in healthcare are the product developers, designers, and marketers of tomorrow. #HealthInnovators who want to win must invite them to be active participants in the #ProductDevelopment process.

_____

_____

_____

117

Many apps, devices, and wearables are brought to market with good intentions of solving real problems, but they don't get any adoption. Part of the problem is a disconnect between the #HealthcareInnovation and patients' needs. #ProductDevelopment

_____

_____

118

Many things get overlooked when you don't involve the right stakeholders in your #Commercialization process. #ProductDevelopment

_____

_____

_____

119

Challenge old traditions around how to solve healthcare problems and how to develop and launch #HealthcareInnovations. #ProductDevelopment

_____

_____

_____

120

#HealthInnovators can be wildly successful if
they make their target markets a part of their
#ProductDevelopment process.

_____

_____

_____

121

Successful #HealthInnovators value stakeholder input in
#ProductDevelopment vs. just getting others to validate
the decisions they've already made.

_____

_____

_____

122

Successful #HealthInnovators look to users and buyers to offer hidden insights, inspire new ideas, bring innovators back to reality, and help position innovations for commercial success. #ProductDevelopment

---

123

Co-creation in #ProductDevelopment is not fast and convenient. If you want a valuable and successful #HealthcareInnovation, take the time to co-create.

124

Developing the right product for the right patient is foundational to healthcare innovation, and tapping into the voice of the patient early is vital to #Commercial success.

_____

_____

_____

125

There are 4 times as many nurses in the healthcare field as doctors, but rarely is their input included in the #ProductDevelopment process. Successful #HealthInnovators don't overlook this segment.

_____

_____

_____

Stay the course —
your friends, family, and
very life may depend on
your #HealthcareInnovation
one day. #Commercializing

DR. ROXIE MOONEY
http://aha.pub/DrRoxieMooney

Share the AHA messages from this book socially by going to
http://aha.pub/HealthcareInnovations.

Section X

Tips to Encourage Health Innovators to Survive

When we think of health innovators—and any startup, for that matter—we think that hard work and perseverance (and maybe being in the right place at the right time) are the key drivers for success. While these ingredients are critical for an innovation to gain momentum and diffuse through the mainstream market, these factors don't guarantee success.

I'm not here to be a harbinger of doom. I am here to help inspire and motivate you toward prosperity and success with a dose of reality and tips to help discouraged health innovators survive and keep going.

"Most great ideas that make it to implementation get killed about three times. Have the patience, the will, and the resources to stay the course."
—*Dr. Robert Groves, Banner-Aetna* *www.drroxie.com/robert*

Watch this video:
http://aha.pub/HealthcareInnovationsS10

126

Your #HealthcareInnovation can drive growth, boost profits, slash competition, and maybe even change the world for the better. Don't give up! #Commercializing

_____

_____

_____

127

You have the opportunity to change the world and save lives. Make sure you #Commercialize your #HealthcareInnovation properly to deliver it to customers who need it.

_____

_____

_____

128

You are the writer of a powerful #HealthcareInnovation story that goes far beyond telling your customers who you are and what you do. Inspire people to buy. #Commercializing

_____

_____

_____

129

Success is not final, failure is not fatal: It is the courage to continue that counts.—Winston Churchill #Commercialize #HealthcareInnovations

_____

_____

_____

130

Stay the course—your friends, family, and very life may depend on your #HealthcareInnovation one day. #Commercializing

_____

_____

_____

131

Give yourself permission to fail, but make sure you learn from it and move forward with your journey to #Commercialize your #HealthcareInnovation.

_____

_____

_____

132

It's better to seek out failure, experience it, and learn from it vs. avoiding failure and wasting time. #Commercializing #HealthcareInnovations

_____

_____

_____

133

I have not failed. I've just found 10,000 ways that won't work.—Thomas Edison #Commercializing #HealthcareInnovations

_____

_____

_____

134

Successful #HealthInnovators surround themselves with people who believe in their vision and say, "It will work out." #Commercializing #HealthcareInnovations

_____

_____

_____

135

Successful #HealthInnovators surround themselves with people who will remind them that no doesn't mean failure, it just means "not yet." #Commercializing #HealthcareInnovations

_____

_____

_____

136

There's no shame in temporarily putting yourself before your #HealthcareInnovation. If you feel overwhelmed, take a breather and some downtime. #Commercializing

_____

_____

_____

137

Developing a self-care plan is as important as #Commercializing your #HealthcareInnovation. Are you taking care of yourself?

_____

_____

_____

138

Perseverance and grit matter more to success than talent. #Commercializing your #HealthcareInnovation is a marathon, not a sprint.

_____

_____

_____

139

Successful #HealthInnovators know that it's important to care for themselves throughout the marathon. They don't just collapse after the initial sprint. They pace themselves. #Commercializing #HealthcareInnovation

_____

_____

_____

140

The journey to #Commercializing your #HealthcareInnovation is difficult. It takes tenacity and perseverance, but it's worth it if people are benefiting from your innovation.

_____

_____

_____

References

Alpert, F., & Saxton, M. K. (2015). Can multiple new-product messages attract different consumer segments? Journal of Advertising Research, 55, 307-321. doi:10.2501/jar-2015-011

Åsberg, P. (2015). Perceived brand portfolios: How individual views hamper efficiency. Journal of Product & Brand Management, 24, 610-620. doi.org/10.1108/jpbm-12-2014-0764

Calantone, R. J., & Di Benedetto, C. A. (2012). The role of lean launch execution and launch timing on new product innovation performance. Journal of the Academy of Marketing Science, 40, 526-538. doi:10.1007/s11747-011-0258-1

Capone, G., Malerba, F., & Orsenigo, L. (2013). Are switching costs always effective in creating first-mover advantage? The moderating role of demand and technological regimes. Long Range Planning, 46, 348-368. doi:10.1016/j.lrp.2013.06.001

Chiesa, V., & Frattini, F. (2011). Commercializing technological innovation: Learning from failures in high-tech markets. Journal of Product Innovation Management, 28, 437-454. doi:10.1111/j.1540-5885.2011.00818.x

Chuang, F. M., Morgan, R. E., & Robson, M. J. (2015). Customer and competitor insights, new product development competence, and new product creativity: differential, integrative, and substitution effects. Journal of Product Innovation Management, 32(2), 175-182. doi.org/10.1111/jpim.12174

Coviello, N. E., & Joseph, R. M. (2012). Creating major innovations with customers: Insights from small and young technology firms. Journal of Marketing, 76(6), 87-104. doi:10.1509/jm.10.0418

Fosfuri, A., Lanzolla, G., & Suarez, F. F. (2013). Entry-timing strategies: The road ahead. Long Range Planning, 46, 300-311. doi:10.1016/j.lrp.2013.07.001

Frattini, F., De Massis, A., Chiesa, V., Cassia, L., & Campopiano, G. (2012). Bringing to market technological innovation: What distinguishes success from failure. International Journal of Engineering Business Management, 4(15), 1-11. doi:10.5772/51605

Fuchs, C., & Diamantopoulos, A. (2012). Customer-perceived positioning effectiveness: Conceptualization, operationalization, and implications for new product innovation managers. Journal of Product Innovation Management, 29, 229-244. doi:10.1111/j.1540-5885.2011.00892.x

Griffin, A., & Page, A. L. (1993). An interim report on measuring product development success and failure. Journal of Product Innovation Management, 10, 291-308. doi:10.1111/1540-5885.1040291

Haavisto, P. (2014). Observing discussion forums and product innovation–A way to create consumer value? Case heart-rate monitors. Technovation, 34, 215-222. doi:10.1016/j.technovation.2013.12.001

Heidenreich, S., & Kraemer, T. (2015). Innovations—Doomed to fail? Investigating strategies to overcome passive innovation resistance. Journal of Product Innovation Management. doi:10.1111/jpim.12273

Heidenreich, S., Wittkowski, K., Handrich, M., & Falk, T. (2014). The dark side of customer co-creation: Exploring the consequences of failed co-created services. Journal of the Academy of Marketing Science, 43, 279-296. doi:10.1007/s11747-014-0387-4

Herhausen, D., Binder, J., Schogel, M., & Herrmann, A. (2015). Integrating bricks and clicks: Retailer-level and channel-level outcomes of online-offline channel integration. Journal of Retailing, 91, 309-325. doi:10.1016/j.jretai.2014.12.009

Hultink, E. J., Griffin, A., Hart, S., & Robben, H. S. (1997). Industrial new product innovation launch strategies and product development performance. Journal of Product Innovation Management, 14, 243-257. doi:10.1111/1540-5885.1440243

Jang, S., & Chung, J. (2015). How do interaction activities among customers and between customers and firms influence market performance and continuous product innovation? An empirical investigation of the mobile application market. Journal of Product Innovation Management, 32, 183-191. doi:10.1111/jpim.12170

Kim, N., Min, S., & Chaiy, S. (2015). Why do firms enter a new product market? A two-dimensional framework for market entry motivation and behavior. Journal of Product Innovation Management, 32(2), 263-278. doi.org/10.1111/jpim.12223

Lévesque, M., Minniti, M., & Shepherd, D. (2013). How late should johnny-come-lately come? Long Range Planning, 46, 369-386. doi:10.1016/j.lrp.2013.06.004

Lieberman, M. B., & Montgomery, D. B. (2013). Conundra and progress: Research on entry order and performance. Long Range Planning, 46, 312-324. doi:10.1177/0149206314563982

López, M., & Sicilia, M. (2013). How WOM marketing contributes to new product innovation adoption: Testing competitive communication strategies. European Journal of Marketing, 47, 1089-1114. doi:10.1108/03090561311324228

Lynch, P., O'Toole, T., & Biemans, W. (2014). From conflict to crisis in collaborative NPD. Journal of Business Research, 67, 1145-1153. doi:10.1111/jpim.12293

Markides, C., & Sosa, L. (2013). Pioneering and first mover advantages: The importance of business models. Long Range Planning, 46, 325-334. doi:10.1016/j.lrp.2013.06.002

Moogk, D. R. (2012). Minimum viable product and the importance of experimentation in technology startups. Technology Innovation Management Review, 2(3), 23-26. Retrieved from http://timreview.ca

Nerkar, A., & Shane, S. (2007). Determinants of invention commercialization: An empirical examination of academically sourced inventions. Strategic Management Journal, 28, 1155-1166. doi:10.1002/smj.643

Ostlund, L. E. (1974). Perceived Innovation Attributes as Predictors of Innovativeness. Journal of Consumer Research, 1(2), 23. https://doi.org/10.1086/208587

Poetz, M. K., & Schreier, M. (2012). The value of crowdsourcing: Can users really compete with professionals in generating new product innovation ideas? Journal of Product Innovation Management, 29, 245-256. doi:10.1111/j.1540-5885.2011.00893.x

Rahman, K., & Areni, C. S. (2014). Generic, genuine, or completely new? Branding strategies to leverage new product innovations. Journal of Strategic Marketing, 22(1), 3-15. doi:10.1080/0965254x.2013.817475

Rasmussen, E. S., & Tanev, S. (2015). The emergence of the lean global startup as a new type of firm. Technology Innovation Management Review, 5(11). doi.org/10.1142/s1363919615400083

Reinhardt, R., & Gurtner, S. (2015). Differences between early adopters of disruptive and sustaining innovations. Journal of Business Research, 68(1), 137-145. doi:10.1016/j.jbusres.2014.04.007

Restuccia, M., Brentani, U., Legoux, R., & Ouellet, J. F. (2015). Product life‐cycle management and distributor contribution to new product development. Journal of Product Innovation Management, 33(1), 69-89. doi.org/10.1111/jpim.12261

Rogers, E. M. (2004). A prospective and retrospective look at the diffusion model. Journal of Health Communication, 9(S1), 13-19. doi:10.1080/10810730490271449

Russo-Spena, T., & Mele, C. (2012). "Five co-s" in innovating: A practice-based view. Journal of Service Management, 23, 527-553. doi:10.1108/09564231211260404

Suarez, F. F., Grodal, S., & Gotsopoulos, A. (2015). Perfect timing? Dominant category, dominant design, and the window of opportunity for firm entry. Strategic Management Journal, 36, 437-448. doi:10.1002/smj.2225

Talke, K., & Snelders, D. (2013). Information in launch messages: Stimulating the adoption of new high-tech consumer products. Journal of Product Innovation Management, 30, 732-749. doi:10.1111/jpim.12017

Theilacker, M., Lukas, B. A., & Snow, C. C. (2016). Potential dimensions of customer co-creation. In looking forward, looking back: Drawing on the past to shape the future of marketing (pp. 218-219). Springer International Publishing. doi:10.1007/978-3-319-24184-5_56

Vidal, E., & Mitchell, W. (2013). When do first entrants become first survivors?. Long Range Planning, 46, 335-347. doi:10.1016/j.lrp.2013.06.006

York, J. L., & Danes, J. E. (2014). Customer development, innovation, and decision-making biases in the lean startup. Journal of Small Business Strategy, 24(2), 21-39. Retrieved from http://www.jsbs.org

Zachary, M. A., Gianiodis, P. T., Payne, G. T., & Markman, G. D. (2014). Entry timing enduring lessons and future directions. Journal of Management, 41, 1388-1415. doi:10.1177/0149206314563982

Appendix A

Develop an Early Adoption Commercialization Strategy to Maximize Market Success

Health innovators want—and need—to know the best strategy to adopt to increase their chances of market success. As health innovators, you have three options. Option 1: Avoid failure. Option 2: Increase your chances of success. Option 3: Maximize market success.

Decipher and Understand the Pyramid of Healthcare Innovation Success

- **Maximizing Market Success**—Thriving. High amounts of short-term satisfaction and a high number of long-term benefits.
- **Increasing Your Chances of Success**—Sustaining. Possibly interesting in the short term, but not particularly rewarding in the long run.
- **Avoiding Failure**—Surviving. Low amounts of short-term satisfaction and a limited number of long-term benefits.

There are many things that can get in the way. What I find again and again is that innovators either confuse or interchange the processes of launch and commercialization, or they focus completely on one and ignore the other. Based on my research and experience, launch and commercialization are different functions of the innovation process.

Launching is a much smaller scale process: it occurs when the innovation is developed and ready for its first release into the market. In the launch process, the goal is to maximize consumer exposure to the innovation through various promotional strategies and distribution channels.

Commercializing is the holistic process of converting ideas, research, and concepts into viable products that obtain consumer acceptance, cross into mainstream adoption, and ultimately generate a financial return on the innovation. Commercialization takes place long before the product is ready to launch and continues long after its initial release. Launching is critical, of course, but it's actually a subset of commercialization.

How does commercialization success tie to market success? It's in who adopts a product and when. My research indicates that success in the mainstream market depends on success with early adopters. If you are not successful with them, you will not be successful over the long term.

Therefore, health innovators must make sure they are not just trying to launch a product but are also developing an early adoption commercialization strategy—a comprehensive business strategy—for how the organization will create, deliver, and capture value, focused specifically on satisfying early adopters.

There are five components required for penetrating the early market: timing, targeting, communication, product, and pilot strategies. How well a company performs in these five areas in the early stages of commercialization will determine if and how they will be successful.

The Five Components of the CoIQ Early Adoption Commercialization Strategy

- Timing strategies
- Targeting strategies
- Communication strategies
- Product strategies
- Pilot strategies

That's why I developed CoIQ. You're probably wondering what "CoIQ" means. CoI stands for Commercialization of Innovation. IQ is for intelligence. Combined, CoIQ reflects my commitment to help health innovators raise their "CoIQ" about what strategies are required to maximize market success of their innovations.

CoIQ is an early adoption commercialization strategy that helps health innovators ensure that they are planning their timing, targeting, communication, product, and pilot strategies. This level of planning is essential to long-term market success.

Many health innovators are happy if they simply avoid failure. The ones who truly make a difference in the market are those who have figured out how to maximize their success.

This book is written for health innovators who want to discover not only how to avoid failure but also how to adopt the key components of an early adoption commercialization strategy. By applying these insights, health innovators will not only increase their chances of success but also ensure that they are making the most of their healthcare innovations.

Together, we will maximize the potential of every new product brought to market and make sure that the latest innovations in healthcare get into the hands of the people who need them most—so we, our families, and our friends live, live longer, and live better.

Appendix B

Wisdom from Some of Healthcare's Brightest Leaders

No single health innovator is going to transform healthcare on their own. If we're going to move the needle, it will require all of us coming together, sharing best practices, and learning from each other. That's why I launched *CoIQ with Dr. Roxie*. It is a first-of-its-kind interactive video and podcast show where top health innovators, early adopters, and influencers speak candidly about their healthcare innovation experiences.

The show is not about promoting new solutions, although sometimes, I cannot help but rave about the amazing ideas our guests are bringing to market. On this show, we discuss why some innovations fail and others succeed, strategies for success, and how our guests overcame the challenges of healthcare commercialization.

I've had the privilege of speaking with some of the industry's brightest healthcare leaders. Here is a snapshot of a few of their AHA statements.

David Goldsmith, WEGO Health	"Consider starting with a patient advisory board to involve patients earlier in the product co-creation process."	www.drroxie.com/david
Dr. Bonnie Clipper, Wambi	"Involve nurses up front in the design and development process to help speed up R&D time and eliminate ideas that won't work."	www.drroxie.com/bonnie
Dr. Joseph Kvedar, Partners Healthcare	"There is a healthcare equivalent to celebrity endorsements. There is a healthcare equivalent to getting buzz on social media. Do not underestimate the value of spending money on PR and marketing, it's really important."	www.drroxie.com/joseph

Dr. Kate Wolin, Coeus Health	"If someone is using a solution that does not work in place of something that we know does, there's a risk there. Evidence is what helps people de-risk."	www.drroxie.com/kate
Dr. Robert Grove, Banner-Aetna	"Most great ideas that make it to implementation get killed about three times. Have the patience, the will, and the resources to stay the course."	www.drroxie.com/robert
John Sharp, Personal Connected Healthcare Alliance	"Providers don't want additional burden, they want to simplify their work and make it more effective. Understand the financial side, as well as the clinical side of their process."	www.drroxie.com/john
Lisa Suennen, Venture Valkyrie	"Appreciate how payments move through the system. There are a lot of people you'll 'touch' in the process before a product gets to a patient."	www.drroxie.com/lisa
Lucia Savage, Omada	"If our products are not grounded in science, then we need to rethink our products. We want to make sure we're improving the healthcare system."	www.drroxie.com/lucia
Matthew Holt, The Healthcare Blog	"Try to identify clearly, to investors and to the buying public, what it is you're doing."	www.drroxie.com/matthew
Robbie Cape, 98point6	"You've got to fail, you've got to learn, you've got to change, and you've got to grow."	www.drroxie.com/robbie
Stacie Ruth, AireHealth	"The team and the process that the team uses to commercialize an innovation is as important as what you're commercializing."	www.drroxie.com/stacie

About the Author

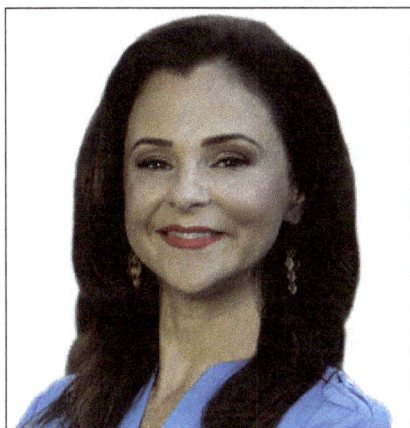

Dr. Roxie Mooney, DBA helps health innovators maximize market success. She combined 20 years in marketing, 10 years as an agency owner, and a doctorate in business that uniquely focuses on healthcare innovation into a blueprint for making commercialization decisions.

It's called the CoIQ Early Adoption Commercialization Strategy, and that's what helps health innovators not only avoid failure but also increase their chances of success and ensure they are making the most of their healthcare innovations.

She also produces and hosts *CoIQ with Dr. Roxie*, a first-of-its-kind interactive video and podcast show where top health innovators, early adopters, and influencers speak candidly about their healthcare innovation experiences. She recently published, "How Leaders Market and Commercialize Healthcare Technology Innovation," in the peer-reviewed *Journal of Business & Economic Perspectives* (JBEP) and is an associate professor at the Jack Welch Management Institute and Palm Beach Atlantic University.

AHAthat®

THiNKaha has created AHAthat for you to share content from this book.

- ➲ Share each AHA message socially:
  http://aha.pub/HealthcareInnovations
- ➲ Share additional content: **https://AHAthat.com**
- ➲ Info on authoring: **https://AHAthat.com/Author**

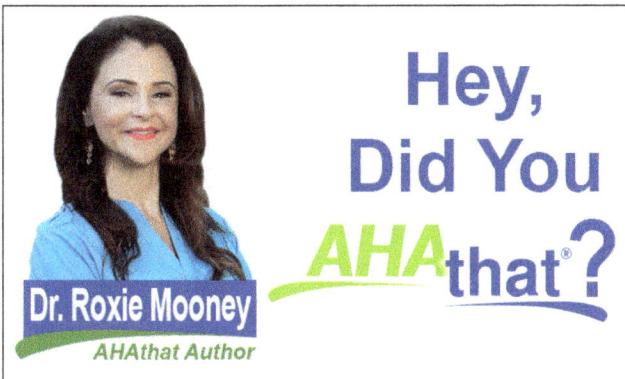

Hey, Did You AHAthat®?

Dr. Roxie Mooney

AHAthat Author